The Imaginary Lighthouse

Vanessa Grant

Presentation by *BookLeaf Publishing*

Web: www.bookleafpub.com

E-mail: info@bookleafpub.com

ISBN: 9789357695459

First edition 2022

To Leon and Isobel,

*Reading and writing are certainly not
boring, hope this helps change your minds
xxx*

ACKNOWLEDGEMENT

I must thank Nikolai, who is never boring to be around.
Mina for the squishy hugs.
And Stuart, for always encouraging me to follow my dreams and desires (even when that's a nap).

Breakfast.

Coffee, hot in pot,
Toast with butter, cereal too,
Time to start the day.

Radiator Socks.

Six o'clock still dark outside,
Under the covers I wish to hide,
Five minutes more, I tell myself,
As I put my phone back on the shelf.

I can hear the wind against the pane,
And the rain running down the drain,
I can see the chill waiting beyond,
The ice atop the garden pond.

Peel the blankets, jump from bed,
Night time garments quickly shed,
Morning's outfit cold as well,
Trying not to touch the material.

Downstairs, the thermometer dial,
dance across the kitchen tiles,
Toast on and porridge hot,
Tea now brewing the pot.

Warmer now than before,
But can't feel my toes any more,
and then a memory doth knocks,
A gift I left me, radiator socks!

Slipping them on is such bliss,
Like a warm and fluffy kiss,
The last of chill chased away,
Now ready to take on the day!

I Miss my Bed.

Streaking through the curtains drawn,
A rude reminder that nights now done,
Such pleasant dreams just can't outrun,
A blinding streak of bright gold sun,
And the house awakes with the dawn.

Muscles tense and eyelids weary,
The day has started it's time to start,
And while at first its hard to part,
from covers deep and full of heart,
The sun shines, ever cheery.

At first like the walking dead,
Muscles stiff and bones that creak,
Catching mirror, all but shriek,
Looking like a used antique,
With a birds nest upon the head.

Nothing a god cuppa won't fix,
Slip downstairs, don't wake the house,
Grab those pants and that clean blouse,
I guess we should though, rouse the spouse,
Tea bag first, hot water then milk and mix.

Two teas' steaming in the mug,
Make the breakfast, no debate,
Children up, or we'll run late,
Children dressed, hair now straight,
Make time for a quick snug.

Everything ready its time to go,
One on shoulders, one holds hands,
On shoulders makes demands,
Holds hands pretends she's in a band,
And both have things they want to show.

At the school they can't wait to start,
The doors open and in they fly,
Not so much as a sweet goodbye,
Underneath the warming sky,
They'll be missed while we're apart.

Right back home and start again,
Plates need washing, clothes to clean,
Toys away so they're unseen,
Hoovering, polishing all routine,
And finally drink; cold, tea then.

Lunch is served, a simple fare,
Then rooms to tidy, beds to make,
Garden tidy, leaves to rake
Perhaps if there's time I'll bake a cake,
Find the socks that make a pair.

School run two, it's time to move,
Children to collect, a kiss on cheek,
It's time to listen about their week,
And wait patiently for a chance to speak,
So we can say how we approve.

In again, time for drinks,
Wind them up and off they go,
Forgetting how to take it slow,
Toys go everywhere clothes are thrown,
I briefly muse what the neighbour thinks.

Not for long, as its time to cook,
Something healthy, tasty too,
It can't be a casserole or a stew,
It can't have mushrooms or 'look blue',
A tricky mission undertook.

Bellies full and getting sleepy now,
Up the stairs for bath and bed,
Two or three books read,
Tuck them in to rest their head,
Slip on out, if they allow.

Tidy up and put away,
Take a breathe and wait and see,
If the children call for me,
If not, then I am free,
It's the end of another day.

Flower Garden.

Doesn't matter if its large,
Very neat or a little wild,
On a rooftop or a barge,
Exotic, exuberant, elegant or mild.

Full of colour or quite plain,
With a place for little souls,
Tricky or easy to maintain,
Or any numerous other goals.

A place to host, relax or to play,
Or to sit and chat with friends,
To just exist and enjoy the day,
To watch the seasons descend,

Whatever way, we can all agree,
A garden is a marvellous place to be.

Happiness.

Hectic adult life might be,
Always rushing too and fro,
Perpetually running low,
Pensive until we're free,
In the evening when it is late,
No distractions to keep us from,
Enjoying hobbies until we succumb,
Slowly, softly, we reach that state,
Sweet, contentment, happiness.

Don't Step on the Cracks.

Walking home from school one day,
A new game he wants to play,
Hopping here and jumping there,
Giggling happily without a care.

He stops a moment, whoa whoa whoa,
A long pause, we wait, then go,
Pointing down at the floor,
At the cracks not there before.

Oh no no no no, he does decry,
We can jump? I do reply,
Off we set, new game and rules,
We don't care if we look the fools.

Laughing, joking having fun,
Spending time just him and mum.

I'd Love to be.

Oh how I'd love to be,
A bright and buzzy, fuzzy bee,
To flit around so gracefully.

Or a cat, with whiskers twitchy,
To sit on laps, or act quite witchy,
And get a brush when I get itchy.

What about a dog named lassie,
Looking elegant and super classy,
And rolling in a patch that's grassy.

I could be a rabbit, fluffy and cute,
With velvet ears and twitchy snoot,
Eating veggies and sometimes fruit.

Or a fish, swimming fast and free,
In the waves of the big blue sea,
No one alive, would ever catch me.

Maybe a tiger, strong and proud,
With a roar that is mighty loud,
Staying away from the crowd.
I could be a bird, singing sweet,
Preening to keep my feathers neat,

Making a twig into my seat.

Oh I could be many things,
With tails, fins or pretty wings,
But then I'd miss what makes us kings,
All the fun and fancy, imagination brings.

Sky on Fire.

Red and pink upon the morning,
Giving out a silent warning,
Not usually an ideal threat,
But of weather that is cold or wet.

Up and up, still quite high,
The clouds that stretch across the sky,
Hues of pink, gold and red,
Conveying things, that can't be said.

Red and orange when it's dusk,
Is considered quite glorious,
A message that is clear in its way,
Of a bright and pleasant day.

A sky so fierce, painted hues,
Orange, Purple, and in blues,
Spreading across a sky so wide,
Offering all a place to hide.

I'm Still a Rebel, Honest.

I no longer wear my thorny crown,
My stompy boots, and slashed up jeans,
I may not wear my make up and a frown,
Or my shirt with the ripped up seams,
But I'm still a rebel, honest.

I may have swapped the bike for a car,
Traded the beer and shots for hot cups of tea,
Prefer to stay at home rather than travel afar,
And replaced my attitude with an honours
degree,
But I'm still a rebel, honest.

I often wonder when its late at night,
If my Mother and Father had it right,
A punk and a rocker when young and free,
That was of course until they had me.
But they were still rebels, honest.

You see, being a rebel is not what you wear,
What you drive or what you drink,
Not how you look or comb your hair,
It is what you say, do and what you think,
So we are rebels, honest.

We dance in the streets regardless who might
see,
We sing in the aisles or wherever we might be,
Life is short and we've only got one,
So we should allow ourselves to have some fun.
Because we are -all- still rebels, honest.

Lunch.

15

Ponder, if you will,
The importance of a meal,
Warmth and gratitude.

A Dream.

It always starts simple, one can't deny,
Walking down a path, winding and low.
Sleepy city, and an overcast sky,
And a cold wind that blows.

A beach to our right but suitcase in hand,
Carry on going, to the place we ought to be?
Or head out over the soft, warm sand?
The beach now in view, where's the sea?

Walking across the soft flat dunes,
A cave to the right some way to go,
And those who like still afternoons,
But no one there you'd know.

Suitcase now has disappeared,
Yet still, nothing feels remiss,
While it should all feel quite weird,
All that looms is a sense of bliss.

The sea now seen, at least a mile away,
A mile back to the gap in the street,
No port, no ship, not even a quay,
No choice now just follow your feet.

Much by surprise, just outside the cave,
The entrance as wide as a lion's maw,
A deep breathe out and feeling brave,
Stepping onto smooth and slippery floor.

Deeper in, the light grows dim,
The walls, jagged, growing close,
Water cold, now swirls around the shin,
A sound inside, like clearing throats.

This place is not what it may seem,
Rational thought, says turn and flee,
However, since this is just a dream,
Further still, the water now at knee.

All too late, the path out is gone,
Forward is the only option left,
Onward and under, now your drawn,
Pray you can hold your breath.

The water cold, or at least you think,
Something still, you can hear,
As you slowly begin to sink,
And the senses begin to clear.

The panic sets in, but still it's weird,
Despite the effort to move you go nowhere,
The end is near, or so is feared,
Despite the screaming, you don't need air.

Drawn down deep by the undertow,
A hand, a face, in the water clear,
Distorted, disjointed by the constant flow,
Alien, beautiful and somehow familiar.

And then awake, in your own bed,
Hands are warm but your feet are cold,
The images still dancing in your head,
On your ankle a handprint, you behold.

Pets.

I think that almost everyone can agree,
What happy memories that can be,
When one gets to play or see,
The love between a pet and thee.

Fluffy, sweet and does sweet tricks,
A scratchy tongue, or smooth that licks,
Can fetch a ball, a treat or sticks,
Furry tail, or scaled that flicks.

Perhaps they have feathers or fur,
Scales or skin, whatever you prefer,
Perhaps they bark, squeak or purr,
Whether they're a mister or a her.

Whether we give them a good brush,
Or have to clean them out in a rush,
Those who sing like a thrush,
And those who to others we like to gush.

Whether they will let us give them pets,
No matter how often they need the vets,
How often we are left to fret,
Or how irritating their behaviour gets.

Snakes, Fish and tortoise, all those in the scaly
crew,
Hamsters, Rats, and gerbils those that love to
chew,
Horses, Chickens, Pigs and Gliders, to name a
few,
Cat's and Dogs, Rabbits, and all the others too.

No matter their looks, we can all agree,
How boring and poor life would be,
Whether we own them, or watch them run free,
Our lives are made better by the pets we get to
see.

Streetlights.

21

Look for the streetlights, their pools of light-
Before the LED's, when they were still bright,
Imagine them as lighthouses, tall and thin,
Promising safe harbour, if you just come in.

Out in the darkness there'd be a stormy sea,
And a pirate captain waiting for thee,
A monster fierce with many arms,
And a mermaid with deadly charms.

The cars that pass by just merchant ship,
The wind that blows, waves that flow and dip,
Hills become islands, and trees sharp rock,
However not here does this ship dock.

Light to light, off we row,
Going fast, or take it slow,
Now it's time homeward go,
Following on the way we know.

Home again and right on time,
Before the eleventh chime.

Leaves in the Wind.

The colours and cascading leaves,
Hues of ruby and gold so at ease,
Back and forth they bob and weave,
Like little dancers in the breeze.

Caught in a draft and up they go,
Disorientated and out of flow,
Oblivious to the audience below,
Come back again to, to and fro.

Hold up! Drama! What is this,
Did old Sycamore just steal a kiss?
From little Elm, is something amiss?
Now Sycamore turns and splits?

Here comes Oak, watch out son,
Sycamore you'd better run,
Elm protests that its all in fun,
Oak decries that they are done.

Now Elm flutters to the ground,
As Sycamore and Oak spin round,
And while at first it seems unsound,
They a rhythm all their own have found.

So Elm now watches from afar,
Dancing away, just as they are,
As Oak and Sycamore say Au revior,
To little Elm who proved Sub-Par.

Dinner.

But I'm hungry, starving time for food, (re: 6, 12
and 18)
I've tried to be patient, but waiting's done,
I hope you don't think I'm being rude. (Re: 9,
15,19)

I've sat at the table, I'm in a good mood,
I've made no mess, my dearest one,
But I'm hungry, starving time for food.

I've cleaned my face, I've stopped the feud,
I've taken care, I didn't run,
I hope you don't think I'm being rude.

I see it cooking, I don't mean to intrude,
I know it's not long since you begun,
But I'm hungry, starving, time for food.

You know the chaos, that may ensue,
I know you've the patience of a nun,
I hope you don't think I'm being rude.

I know I might be sounding crude.
I'm sorry dad, I'm sorry mum,
But I'm hungry, starving time for food,
I hope you don't think I'm being rude.

Thunderstorm.

25

The sky grows dark, the air is thick,
The wind grows still, there is no sound,
And a feeling stirs all around,
Something primal and almost magic.

It starts at first with a faint rumble,
The animals all go away to sleep,
As the sky begins to weep,
Although it starts off very humble.

A feeling builds, quietly excited,
Waiting for the first clear sign,
Of the storm, a force divine,
Ready and waiting to be delighted.

A flash of light, a deafening crack,
A signal for the rain to start,
Falling hard as heavens part,
The sky above now jet black.

Setting, snug into window seat,
Eyes upturned to watch the clouds,
Of which the heavy rain now shrouds,
Waiting for a brilliant repeat.

Lightning arcs across the sky,
Thunder booms the ground downs rumble,
A booming voice, an old man's grumble,
And the rain a heavy burdened sigh.

And so it goes, for time unknown,
Booming, Rumbling, Hissing past,
Filling a sky so large and vast,
But weather like this is just on loan.

All too soon the rain does cease,
The wind picks up, the lightning gone,
In its wake a new eve dawns,
Fresher, cooler, more at peace.

Oh No!

While cooking dinner all is calm,
This itself should raise alarm,
But this chance is so rare,
To not use it would be unfair,
Pushing away my concern,
Over reacting? Will I never learn.

Everything prepped, just in time,
Still its quiet, that can't be mine,
Loud and proud, cheeky and loud,
Explorer's, discoveries, and often bold,
Mess-makers, decorators, risk takers,
Nerve janglers and shakers.

Rush back now, the front room,
Mess and mayhem, we assume,
Instead curled up like a small cat,
Tucked in blankets, toy on lap,
All snug and warm, asleep it seems,
Having seemingly pleasant dreams.

So for a while, just stand and stare,
At the angels just napping there,
With cute curls, and little toes,
Soft fingers, a button nose,

A sight so bright it fills your heart,
Ignoring the mess they call art.

Alas though, they will soon awake,
Despite the pleasant mini-break,
It's dinner time and then it's bed,
So first they should be well fed,
Just hold that image, keep in mind,
The angels here, when they're hard to find.

A Hug is Enough.

If you've had a day that's rough,
feeling sad or feeling rough,
Stuck on a problem that's quite tough,
Sometimes, a hug is just enough.

If you're angry, lonely, mad,
Or happy, joyful and quite glad,
If you're grieving a hard day had,
Sometimes, a hug is not so bad.

If you've missed them, or been away,
Or you're saying goodbye for the day,
If you've run out of nice things to say,
Sometimes, a hug all this will convey.

Hugs are warm, soft and kind,
They warm a place that's hard to find,
They say words that can't be defined,
So give them a hug; if you're so inclined.

Of course if a hug for you is hard,
How about a letter, picture or card?
A gift, or act to show you're regard,
Because sometimes, a hug is not enough.

Oil Stain, Oil Stain on the Wall.

Oil stain, oil stain upon the wall,
Why do you prevent me sleeping at all?
Don't you know you scare my kid?
Who has flipped on the lights and run and hid.

Dirty clothes, dirty clothes on the floor,
Don't you know I want to sleep and snore?
Why do you take form late at night?
And give my kids an awful fright?

Scurrying creatures in the dark,
I know you think it's all a lark,
but I'm sat up with lights turned on,
trying to convince her that nothings wrong.

Whispering winds through the street,
Sweeping leaves across concrete,
I know you're just doing you,
But to her you might as well be saying BOO!

It's morning now, the dawn is here,
And in the light she has no fear,
But another night without sleep,
As to her this promise I always keep.

That in the night if nightmares come,
I'll chase them back where they're from,
I'll stay with her the whole night through,
Until the shadows have shrunk, withdrew.

I'll be there to keep her calm,
To hold her close and safe from harm,
I'll be brave for her until she too can see,
It's just a stain, clothes and trees.

Because when I was little just like she,
My imagination ran away with me,
It made witches, demons and monsters as well,
Night would be my personal hell.

And my dad, smooth as can be,
Would take my hand and sit with me,
He'd keep me safe until morning light,
Even if it meant staying up all night.

And perhaps one day, in a future to come,
When my daughter is an aunt or mum,
She too will sit all night with a small tot,
Fighting monsters for the she she loves a lot.

Five Minutes Peace.

Day is drawing to a close,
Dishes done, you've washed the clothes.
Hoovering finished and noses wiped,
Kids tucked in for the night.
Memories of the day gone past,
Everything happening all too fast.

Dressed and ready, out the door,
Get back home to mop the floor.
Out for shopping, not for fun,
Forgot the tea for dad and mum.
Check through mail, watch the news,
No time today for your running shoes.
Lunchtime rush to get refuelled,
Despite different directions you are pulled.
Fold the clothes, but wait. You're pretty sure,
That odd sock had a pair before!
Wipe the surfaces, clean the bath,
And right about now you've had enough.
No time now, time is moving on,
Almost time to collect the spawn.
And of course it's raining, that's alright,
The kids all screaming with pure delight.
Avoid the puddles, no, through them, fine,
Back indoors and they begin to whine.

Coats all hung and shoes away,
Time to tackle the last mission of the day.
Chopped, sliced, stirred and in the pot,
Dinner prepared but nerves well shot.
Served at table, eaten in lounge,
With the dogs a-hoping to scrounge.
Homework finished, up for a bath,
Distract the children make them laugh.
Kids all clean and tucked in tight,
Story told and kissed goodnight.

Not a sound as bath was run,
All is silent, every one.
And as the bubbles hug away,
The stresses of a busy day.
From down the hallway, behind the door,
You swear you hear footsteps on the floor.

Ignore it all. For five minutes peace?
Perhaps they'll simply stop and cease.
"MUM!"
Oh well, there's always tomorrow right?

Dessert.

34

Pudding tasty, sweet and hot,
In a bowl, on a plate or not,
From the oven, in a pot,
Creamy or crunchy I'll have the lot!